MACHINES AT WORK

Cars

Clive Gifford

 Crabtree Publishing Company

www.crabtreebooks.com

Crabtree Publishing Company
www.crabtreebooks.com
1-800-387-7650

PMB 59051, 350 Fifth Ave.   616 Welland Ave.
59th Floor,   St. Catharines, ON
New York, NY 10118   L2M 5V6

Published by Crabtree Publishing in 2013

Author: Clive Gifford
Editors: Nicola Edwards, Adrianna Morganelli
Proofreaders: Wendy Scavuzzo, Crystal Sikkens
Designer: Elaine Wilkinson
Picture Researcher: Clive Gifford
**Production coordinator and
    Prepress technician**: Ken Wright
Print coordinator: Katherine Berti

To find out about the author, visit his website:
www.clivegifford.co.uk

First published in 2012 by Wayland
(A division of Hachette Children's Books)
Copyright © Wayland 2012

Printed in Hong Kong/ 092012/BK20120629

Picture acknowledgements:
The author and publisher would like to thank
the following agencies and people for allowing
these pictures to be reproduced:
Cover (main) Max Earey / Shutterstock.com,
(inset) Calvin Chan / Shutterstock.com; title
page 3777190317 / Shutterstock.com; pp2-3
SÃ¡gi ElemÃ©r/Shutterstock.com; p4 Deep-
Green/Shutterstock.com; p5 (t) iStock © Ivan
Cholakov, (b) iStock © Caboclin; p6 © George
Tiedemann/GT Images/Corbis; p7 iStock ©
Lisa Christianson; p8 Jaggat / Shutterstock.com;
p9 (t) Shutterstock © Oskar Calero, (b) © Foto
Huebner/dpa/Corbis; p10 3777190317 / Shut-
terstock.com; p11 (t) iStock © Richard Lau-
rence, (b) cjmac / Shutterstock.com; p12 SÃ¡gi
ElemÃ©r / Shutterstock.com; p13 Shutterstock
© Vitaly Chernyshenko; p14 Michael Stokes /
Shutterstock.com; p15 Thinkstock; p16 Max
Earey / Shutterstock.com; p17 (t) Shutterstock
© Gravicapa, (b) Walter G Arce / Shutterstock.
com; p18 (t) Daimler AG, (b) AFP/Getty Im-
ages; p19 Thinkstock; p20 AFP/Getty Images;
p21 (t) Shutterstock © JustAsc, (b) iStock ©; p22
Daimler AG; p23 (t) DeepGreen/Shutterstock.
com, (b) 3777190317 / Shutterstock.com; p24
Michael Stokes / Shutterstock.com

**Library and Archives Canada
Cataloguing in Publication**

CIP available at Library and Archives Canada

**Library of Congress
Cataloging-in-Publication Data**

CIP available at Library of Congress

Contents

Cars on the move

A car is a vehicle that runs on wheels. An **engine** burns **fuel** and provides the power to make the car's wheels rotate. As the wheels turn, they move the car forward.

Hood—covers the engine beneath

Cars are made up of thousands of parts. They are put together in a factory. The cars are tested to make sure they are safe to drive.

Wheel covered in a rubber tire

ZOOM IN

Engines heat up when the fuel burns inside them. A spinning fan at the front of the engine forces air from outside over the engine to keep it cool.

Some cars such as police cars or cars used by people with disabilities, can be adapted to suit the needs of the people using them.

Trunk—used for storage

Cars can be fitted with lifts to help people who use wheelchairs to get inside.

FAST FACT

There are over 600 million cars being driven on roads all over the world.

Get set, go!

A car's journey begins when the driver starts the engine. A car needs a lot of power from its engine to start moving.

Cars pull away at the start of a race. Each driver tries to make their car go fast enough to take the lead.

FAST FACT

Some racing cars can go from standing still to 100 miles per hour (160 kilometers per hour) in less than a second!

The driver uses a key to start the car's engine. When the engine starts, fuel pumps in and is burned to generate power.

ZOOM IN

A car has different gears. A low gear is used when a car starts moving. It turns the car's wheels slowly but with great force. As the car speeds up, the gears change automatically or by the driver using the gear shift.

Steering a car

The driver moves the car in the direction he or she wants to go by using the **steering** wheel. Moving the steering wheel causes the car to turn left or right or travel around corners and bends in the road.

Crash helmet—protects the driver's head

Driver's hands grip the steering wheel

Engine

A racing **kart** has a small engine but, because it is light in weight, it can still travel fast. The driver has to steer the kart quickly and accurately through all the bends and turns on the track.

ZOOM IN

A car's steering wheel is connected to the front wheels. Turning the steering wheel moves the front wheels so that they point in the same direction as the steering wheel.

Drivers slow their cars down as they enter into a bend. If a driver takes a corner too fast, there is a risk that the car might spin out of control and go off the road or even flip over. The cars can speed up again as they leave the bend.

These race car drivers slow their cars down to keep them under control when going around a bend.

Driver number

Front wheels point left as the kart turns to the left

Front bumper—protects driver's feet

Staying on track

When things rub together, they create a force called **friction**. This slows things down but it also provides grip. Car tires use friction to grip the road or track.

Driver sits in cockpit

The front and rear **wings** on a Formula One racing car create a force that presses the car down onto the track.

Rear wing

Front wing

ZOOM IN

These racing tires are kept warm in a heated blanket. Warmer tires are stickier and grip the track better.

During a race, the tires wear down and have to be replaced. The cars drive off the track and into the pits to get new tires and more fuel. In a blur of action, the pit crew finishes these jobs in less than seven seconds!

Narrow body slices through air

Wide tires grip track

During a **pit stop**, the pit crew races to get a car back on the track as quickly as possible.

Off-road driving

Some cars need to be able to drive off smooth-surfaced roads to travel on muddy, sandy, or snowy ground. These off-road cars are built to be tough because the ground they travel on can be rough and very bumpy.

Co—driver helps keep the car on the right route

Race number

FAST FACT

Every year, hundreds of vehicles take part in a cross-country race called the Dakar Rally. The race lasts three weeks!

A rally car sends up a cloud of dust as it races over rough ground during an off-road race.

ZOOM IN

Off-road cars have tires with a chunky surface pattern. This helps them grip the ground.

Off-road cars have a frame of metal tubes inside to make them stronger. This frame is called a **roll cage**. It protects the driver if the car rolls over onto its side or roof.

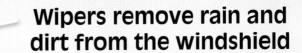

Wipers remove rain and dirt from the windshield

Powerful headlights for seeing through fog, clouds of dust, and at night

Thick rubber tires

Speeding up

To make a car go faster, a driver presses a foot pedal called the **accelerator**. This makes the engine work harder to turn the car's wheels faster.

Driver wears a crash helmet

Small front wheels guide the dragster along the track

Long, thin body slices through the air

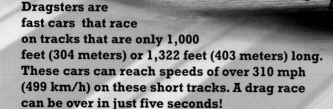

Dragsters are fast cars that race on tracks that are only 1,000 feet (304 meters) or 1,322 feet (403 meters) long. These cars can reach speeds of over 310 mph (499 km/h) on these short tracks. A drag race can be over in just five seconds!

The lights on top of this police car flash as the car speeds to the scene of a crime.

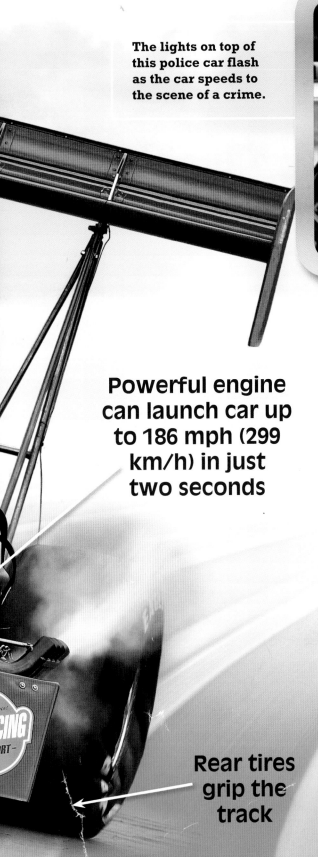

Powerful engine can launch car up to 186 mph (299 km/h) in just two seconds

Rear tires grip the track

Police cars often have to travel faster than other cars on the road. They use flashing lights and a siren to warn other road users that they need to pass.

FAST FACT

The world's fastest police car is the Lamborghini Gallardo, which can reach a top speed of 192 mph (309 km/h).

Slowing down

When drivers want to slow down or stop, they press the car's brake pedal. This makes brake pads press onto a disk inside each wheel. The rubbing of the pads on the disks creates friction, which slows down the car's wheels.

FAST FACT

The brakes in a Bugatti Veyron can slow the car down from 62 mph (100 km/h) to standing still in less than two and a half seconds.

Brakes are fitted inside each wheel

Wheels turn fast until brakes are used

ZOOM IN

When the brakes are used, brake lights at the back of the car shine red. This tells drivers behind that the car ahead is slowing down.

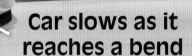

Car slows as it reaches a bend

Dragsters travel so fast, and have to stop so quickly, that ordinary brakes are not enough. Parachutes open behind a dragster and fill with air. This creates a force that pulls the car backward. The force, known as drag, helps to slow the dragster down.

A parachute opens to slow down a dragster at the end of a race.

Different fuels

A car's engine needs fuel for it to work. Most engines use gasoline or diesel fuels made from oil. When these fuels are burned in an engine, they can send harmful gases into the air. Scientists are now working on other, cleaner ways of powering cars.

Low energy lights

This strange-looking car works with solar power.

Some cars are fitted with electric motors that are powered by electricity from sunlight. **Solar panels** on the car turn energy from the Sun into electricity.

ZOOM IN

When the **battery** pack runs down, the driver plugs the car in to recharge it.

electric drive

This Mercedes SmartFortwo car is powered by an electric motor. The motor gets electricity from a large battery pack stored inside the car.

Car holds driver and one passenger

Battery fits in floor of car. Electric motor turns rear wheels to drive the car forward

FAST FACT

In 2004, a car powered by sunlight made a record-setting journey of 9,364 miles (15,070 km) across North America.

Driving safely

Cars are built and tested to keep the people who travel in them safe. When a new type of car is designed, it is crashed in the testing lab to see how it will protect its driver and passengers. Experts study how full-sized models of people, called **crash test dummies**, move around during the crash.

Dummy thrown forward by impact

Airbag

Front of cars crumple when they hit each other

Two cars are crashed together in a safety lab to find out what adjustments need to be made to improve car safety.

ZOOM IN

Seat belts stop you from being forced forward in a crash and hitting your head. Always fasten your seat belt when you travel in a car.

Forces from the crash are absorbed by, or go into, the car's frame

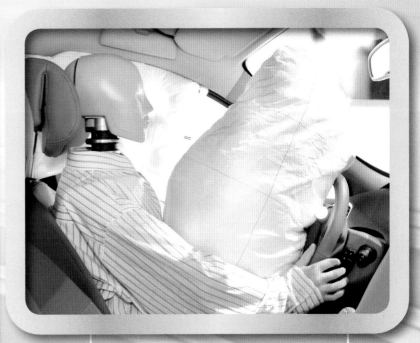

An airbag inflates to stop the crash test dummy from hitting the car's windshield.

When a crash happens, airbags blow up like balloons in a fraction of a second. They cushion the driver's and passenger's faces and upper bodies from injury.

Quiz

How much have you found out about how cars work? Try this short quiz!

1. What part of a car keeps a driver and passengers in their seats?
a) roll cage
b) seat belt
c) airbag

2. What force helps dragsters slow down?
a) drag
b) downforce
c) friction

3. Which foot pedal do drivers press to speed up a car?
a) brake
b) accelerator
c) clutch

4. Many electric cars store energy in what device?
a) battery
b) gears
c) airbags

5. What force slows things down and provides grip?
a) g-force
b) drag
c) friction

6. If you turn a car's steering wheel to the left, in which direction will the car go?
a) right
b) left
c) straight forward

7. Where are the brakes found on a car?
a) hood
b) wheels
c) engine

electric drive

Answers: 1.b, 2.a, 3.b, 4.a, 5.c, 6.b, 7.b

Glossary

accelerator A foot pedal that is pressed down to make the car go faster

battery A device that supplies power to parts of a car such as its lights

bumper A bar made of metal, plastic, or rubber that stops damage to the car if it bumps into something

crash helmet A protective covering worn on the head by race car drivers to stop head injuries if they crash

crash test dummy A full-sized model of a person that is used to test how safe a vehicle is

engine The machinery that creates power to turn the car's wheels

friction The force that slows movement between two objects that rub together

fuel Gasoline, diesel, or another substance burned in an engine to create power to make a car move

hood A body panel on a car that lifts up to reveal the engine

kart A small vehicle that is raced on racetracks for fun or in competitions

pit stop A break during a race when a car leaves the track for repairs, extra fuel, or new tires

roll cage A frame of metal tubes inside a car that protects people if the car rolls onto its side or roof

solar panel A special panel that converts sunlight into electricity to power electric motors in a solar-powered vehicle

steering Controlling a car by making the wheels turn in a specific direction

wings Parts on racing cars and some sports cars that help press the car downward so it grips the track or ground

Further information

Books

Formula One, Adrianna Morganelli, Crabtree Publishing, 2007
NASCAR, Rachel Eagen, Crabtree Publishing, 2007
Sweet Rides, Katharine Bailey, Crabtree Publishing, 2007

Websites

Museo Stradale: http://museostradale.com/Online_Auto_Museum.htm
Photographs and information for more than 90 high-end vintage cars.

DragList.com: www.draglist.com/drlpicture.htm
Hundreds of photographs of dragsters and drag races.

NHRA Drag Racing 101: www.nhra.net/basics/basics.html
A description of the rules of drag racing.

World Karting: www.worldkarting.com/index.php/news/new-to-karting-main *How to get involved in kart racing. Also has three kart racing videos in the "Media" section.*